Packing Light

NEW AND SELECTED POEMS BY
MARILYN KALLET

INTRODUCTION BY ANDY BRUMER

BOOKS BY MARILYN KALLET

Circe, After Hours (poetry)

Last Love Poems of Paul Eluard (translations, two editions)

The Movable Nest: A Mother/Daughter Companion (with K.S. Byer)

Jack the Healing Cat

The Art of College Teaching: 28 Takes (with A. Morgan)

One For Each Night: Chanukah Tales and Recipes

Sleeping With One Eye Open: Women Writers and the Art of Survival
   (with J. O. Cofer)

How to Get Heat Without Fire (poetry)

Worlds in Our Words: Contemporary American Women Writers
   (with P. Clark)

A House of Gathering: Poets on May Sarton's Poetry

Honest Simplicity in William Carlos Williams' "Asphodel, That Greeny Flower"

In the Great Night (poetry)

Devils Live So Near (poetry)

Packing Light

NEW AND SELECTED POEMS BY
MARILYN KALLET

INTRODUCTION BY ANDY BRUMER

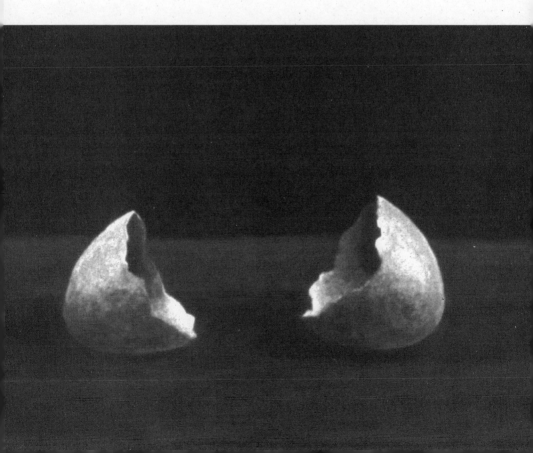

PACKING LIGHT: New and Selected Poems ©2009 Marilyn Kallet. Black Widow
Press thanks the following presses for allowing us to reprint previously published
materials: BkMk Press for excerpts from *Circe, After Hours* ©2005, New Messenger
Books for excerpts from *How to Get Heat Without Fire* ©1996, and Ithaca House for
excerpts from *In the Great Night* ©1981 and *Devils Live So Near* ©1977. Introduction ©2008
Andy Brumer.

Black Widow Press is an imprint of Commonwealth Books, Inc., Boston, MA.
Distributed to the trade by NBN (National Book Network) throughout North
America, Canada, and the U.K. All Black Widow Press books are printed on acid-free
paper, and glued and sewn into bindings. Black Widow Press and its logo are regis-
tered trademarks of Commonwealth Books, Inc.

Black Widow Press would like to thank the University of Tennessee Humanities
Initiative for their support of this title.

Joseph S. Phillips, Publisher
www.blackwidowpress.com

Book and Cover Design: Kerrie Kemperman
Cover Art: Suzanne Stryk

ISBN-13: 978-0-9818088-02
ISBN-10: 0-9818088-0-8

Library of Congress Cataloging-in-Publication Data on file

Kallet, Marilyn, 1946–

Printed by Friesens
Printed in Canada

10 9 8 7 6 5 4 3 2 1

ACKNOWLEDGEMENTS

The following poems have been published in magazines
or anthologies. Grateful acknowledgement is made to the
editors:

Jonah on Oprah, Dear Swallowed, You Weren't There,
 Prairie Schooner
Father Trey Makes an Offer, *Low Explosions*
Charon, With Dignity, At Bikernieki, *Potomac Review*
Two More Gorillas, *The Southern Quarterly*
Tell Yourself, Even This, *The Pinch*
Is There Lightning on Venus, *Gargoyle*
Packing Light, Apology, *Arts & Letters*
Ode to What Cannot Be Praised, *New Millennium Writings*
Hooked, *Caduceus*
Question After the Poetry Reading, *New Letters*
Ode to the Open Window, Madame Assen Remembers,
 Our Man, *New Works Review*
Passport Control, Survivor, *Shirise*

Many of these poems were written with grants from the
Hodges Fund of the English Department at the University
of Tennessee, and with professional development funding
from the Graduate School. A grant from the University
of Tennessee Humanities Initiative helped to support this
project's completion. The Virginia Center for the Creative
Arts in Sweet Briar and in Auvillar, the Mary Anderson
Center for the Arts, and Squaw Valley Community of Writers
continue to be my poetry homes. The United States embassy
in Poland hosted my poetry readings in 2006 through an
invitation from Ambassador Victor Ashe. X.J. Kennedy,
Julia Demmin, Alice Friman, Kali Meister, Barbara Bogue,
and Arthur Smith have encouraged my work throughout the
years. Robert Stewart at *New Letters* wisely edited "Questions

After the Poetry Reading." My publisher Joe Phillips at
Black Widow Press has provided astute editorial advice and
steady encouragement.

And I am grateful to Ben Furnish at BkMk Press, for
permission to reprint poems from *Circe, After Hours*, 2005.
Poems from *How to Get Heat Without Fire*, New Messenger Books,
first appeared in 1996. Selected early poems were reprinted
from *In the Great Night*, 1981, and *Devils Live So Near*, 1977, Ithaca
House.

The original version of Andy Brumer's essay, "Meeting
in Love & Loss," appeared in *Poetry Flash* Fall 2007/Winter
2008. Thanks to him and to Joyce Jenkins at *Poetry Flash* for
permission to excerpt and reprint.

For Lou and Heather, always

In the shelter of our walls
ours is a human door.

—Eluard

TABLE OF CONTENTS

III. CURRENTS

~*from* CIRCE, AFTER HOURS~

~*from* How to Get Heat Without Fire~

~Early Poems~

MEETING IN LOVE & LOSS:
MARILYN KALLET'S POETRY

Marilyn Kallet opens *Circe, After Hours,* her fourth collection
of poems, with this epigraph from the French Surrealist poet,
Paul Eluard: "The sea is cold without love," which is fitting,
as she is also a brilliant translator of Eluard's work. Indeed,
Kallet holds nothing back in striving to rebalance this merci-
less equation, with her warm-bodied poems that loosen fear's
frigidity, and free life's feeling and flow. Poetry flies out
of Kallet and into the world via the centrifugal force of an
indefatigable spirit, and it has been doing so for a long time.
Kallet's poetry intelligently takes the best from the American
modernist and postmodernist grains: Williams's comfortable
and lapidary vernacularism, the confessionalist's self-
examination and exposure, the Beat's leftist stance, spiritual
howls and longing for transcendence. Her poems present a
sense of humor that never settles for facile punchlines but
works dynamically to mine the ironic out of the ordinary-
seeming.

   The humor masks self-deprecating wounds, as in "No
Makeup:" "Makeup can only do so much," the high-priced
cosmetic guru pronounces at the narrator's "wedding consul-
tation." The snide comment strikes home, but, over time, the
poet transforms the blow into a vocation and a gift. Older,
more confident now, she relies on art, not on surfaces,
affirming,

> how, at fifty, I love
> nakedness
> in my face and lines,
> and in your hands, dear reader.

Kallet seems completely at home working within a kind of loosely knit, if not illusorily narrative structure, in which she shatters the logic-bound progression of a story and mines it for its lyrical acoustics and fresh insights and ideas. Her poems possess the energy of de Kooning's portraits of women, where the artist disguises and distorts his figures inside swirling cocoons of energetic paint.

In "Trout," and "No Sale," Kallet shifts lithely into rhapsodic and quirky dissertations on the cultural roots of, odd as it sounds, Jewish sexual fantasy. "No Sale" finds the narrator cleverly positioning the guitar of a famous blues musician both as his literal instrument and as an organ of desire:

> How would a Jewish girl
> sell her soul to the devil?
> Reformed don't believe
> in Beelzebubba.
>
> Now Robert Johnson, he
> had no such trouble.
> You know the tale, how the bluesman
> sold his soul at the crossroads
>
> for a lifetime of hot-lick guitar.

Kallet plays her sense of humor as if it were a musical instrument that shapes the disjunctive and staccato rhythms and the sounds of her words into meditations often both whimsical and sad.

The theme of archaic ghosts, the ubiquity of the dead signaling their unfinished business on earth in poems such as "With Dignity" and "Finally" double dramatically as a metaphorical setup for poems that usher the reader into one of the darkest closets of human history.

The following, from "Survivor," one of several poems about the Holocaust, is so heartbreakingly somber that it subjugates Kallet's protean imagination to a litany of dirge-like statements:

> The Night of Broken Glass,
> thugs set fire to the Rexingen synagogue.
> Scorched the Torah.
> Officials blamed "outsiders."
> Or kindergartners playing with matches.

The poet listens to the past, restoring names and narratives to the voiceless. In bearing equal witness to the comic and tragic, the quotidian and the extraordinary, Kallet's poems trace and celebrate life's spiritual struggle and grace it with an eternal glow.

Ultimately, Kallet's and Eluard's poetry meet in the shared belief that love alone holds humankind's best chance for regeneration, rejuvenation, and joy. "Beneath the dark floor there has always been love," the poet asserts in "How to Get Heat Without Fire," and she invites, coaxes, tenderly or play-fully insists on freeing its sounds and rhythms, making them accessible to a wide community of readers.

—Andy Brumer

Andy Brumer is a poet and essayist, art critic, and reviewer of literature. His recent book is The Poetics of Golf, *University of Nebraska Press.*

NEW POEMS

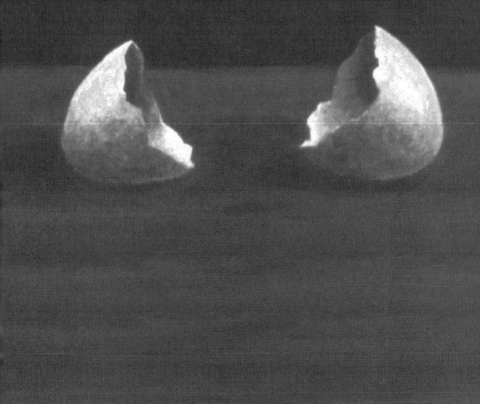

I.

DEAR SWALLOWED

JONAH ON OPRAH

"I've lived through gut-wrenching
remorse, got swallowed up by it.

Now I understand I can't run
from my problems.

I bear witness, whales blow
worse blubber-breath than my boss,

all undigested krill!
I pay attention,

take my medication,
do as told.

I've boarded up the souvenir shop
in Ninevah. No more scrimshaw.

Whales endangered.
I'm not gloating.

I water my spindly plants
until I near-drown them.

Voices?   Only on the tube.
I prefer Law and Order,

and though she's abrasive
as the Negev, Judge Judy.

I just love watching idiots scramble,
try to argue, try to flee!"

DEAR SWALLOWED

If the
low heavy
cover
seems to surround you

you may be trapped
inside a large mammal.
First, check to see
if this is

a metaphor:
can you gasp?
Do you spot sky
through a blowhole?

If yes,
then we recommend
the Pinocchio
pepper spray.

Your cover's
blown
in a good way.
If dry land

also weighs down
then you may be
locked
in the grip of long ennui.

Wellbutrin
will ease
the blubbery aftertaste
the spleenish

hangover you think of
as being—
without sexual side effects.
As if, at your age.

Caution: do not drive
if you're Ishmael
and Ahab's in back
on his cell

trailed by copfish.
You're moseying
the white whale
down the Alameda freeway.

PACKING LIGHT

When I said I wanted to travel light,
didn't mean I'd part with undies
and mascara. That all my baggage

should go missing. When the airline
rang my hotel with "sorry,"
I started making excuses—

"Won't be able to attend
the writers' conference after all,
medical reasons, my heart, etc."

When the Buddha realized
he'd lost everything,
that we were born to die,

he stopped desiring.
(*Nu*, Grandma Anna would have asked,
was he Jewish?)

But the female bodhisattvas
wrapped in silk, swirled
beneath headdresses

that rivaled *Yerushalayim*.
Not so the *mishpokah*.
Grandma in the shtetl,

cousins becalmed
by the Schwarzwald
were forced to let go.

My parents clung hard
to their houses,
cars, and daughters.

Which begs the question,
Marilyn, what ghosts can you pack off,
pitch over the side?

What will you take with you
into your 60th year?
Hanging here

like a little spider,
lightness feels pretty good,
no? Even with the dark

gulping around you.

TWO MORE GORILLAS SENT FROM CHICAGO

This ode's for you, Bengati
and Jelani, newest boys
at the Louisville Zoo.

I don't blame you
for scrapping with that
bully, JoJo, mob ape

from Chi. Old Silverback,
he claimed the turf
and broad for himself.

Long John Silver,
I knew a guy like that.
His silver fur bristled

when a new kid
probed the poetry pack.
She suffered bumps

and bruises,
he trashed her work,
"mere free verse."

She rammed cold triads
up his ass.
Change

can make us glad,
Bengati, Jelani.
Here's to you, new hunks

at the Louisville Zoo!
Have a ball this weekend
with the Monkees

and King Kong,
local boy band
at your welcome bash.

One day you'll both be
good ol' backs,
but for now, cling

to hope:
JoJo will be dead
sooner than you.

PIUS WITH HICCUPS

From the journal of occulist Riccardo Galeazzi-Lisi

"Prelate Eugenio first consulted me
for specs in 1929.

I predicted he'd be Pope.
We hit it off.

When he confided about gas,
I took pity.

Did I claim to be a doctor?
No matter. My advice worked.

When he became Pius XII he invited me
to the Papal City, made me Archistre, Senior

Physician, named to the Academy of Sciences
in Rome. Gave me rooms with a flush

commode. I treated him with paregoric,
revved Kool-Aid with nutmeg and cocaine.

How was I to know that his teeth would rot,
the spices would trigger hiccups?

I wasn't much longer for the papal payroll,
so I installed a line to Reuters

in Castelgandolfo, by the Holy See's bed.
Took a few home movies of his agonies.

I knew *Life Magazine* would bite.
When I offered free embalming, good for

100 years, not one bishop said no.
I bagged his Holiness in cellophane.

Could I foresee his skin would go Frankenstein
from swabs of oil and basil?

He had asked for traditional dressing
in his will. When he turned grey-purple,

Paris Match paid through the nose.
In the October sun en route to St. Peter's,

monster farts and eructations issued
from the coffin. *Merda!* I didn't remove

his intestines. They had to switch
the puking Swiss guards every fifteen minutes.

Culos! We all die, *signore e
signori!* And a blessed patsy is born.

My descendants are still trying to clear the air.
Big deal, I droppered a little dope

in the pope's *vino.* He needed a pick-me-up.
Non me rompere le palle!

Who croaks from hiccups?
Don't break my balls!"

FATHER TREY MAKES AN OFFER

At the friary lunch Father Trey asks,
"Do you have laundry?"
Lean, young Kevin Costner.
We three women poets nod.
"I'd be happy to do your wash," he says.
"Leave it on the porch."

When he leaves we gasp,
"Oh my God!"
Margie whispers red panties.
Jill has been lounging in pink
polka-dotted birthday jammies.
No, no, no, Father Trey.
You will not be handling my
black Barely There bra.

You will not fold my blue
silk bikini bottoms.
You stride like Bull Durham,
Father, and looks
rarely deceive.
What penance makes you seek
soiled underthings?

If you insist,
we could go down
to the nunnery basement
with its old vibrating
wash and spin,
gas-fired pilot lights,
huge hot dryers,
lie on the sturdy table for folding

holy briefs
on top of immaculate towels,
bathe each other with caresses
beneath the hanging jello mold
of our Mother of Consolation.

We'd weep mutual tears of absolution
below the "Cup of Joy" blessing card,
and—you know what's coming—
cleanse each other deeply
with Judeo-Christian tongues.

TELL YOURSELF

He's not the source,
not fat with poems like a cat who
gulped the sun.

Tell yourself he's not a walking love note
from Eros, not sporting purple silk,
hothouse iris.

You don't need the violet surge.
Tell yourself you're enough,
enough!

Sixty years old
in your black bra,
you're not bait anymore.

He surges and ebbs
like seafoam that remembers
the wave

the whale belly the champagne,
spitting you out.
He's Trickster,

gourmet caterer
at the writers' feast,
and Sweetie, you have to eat!

IS THERE LIGHTNING ON VENUS?

Some satellite radios have picked up static.
Others haven't.

Some people sleep through sex but that
doesn't mean it isn't happening

to someone. Someone's ex. Or someone's self,
beneath the comforter of marriage.

Venus nestles the moon in the late spring sky.
When was the last time lightning slapped?

When you turned your back
for a moment on your respectable life

and glimpsed Eros. He grinned.
Two years of a passion that dwarfed your life.

Some radios don't get it.
At sixty, don't replace them.

What you're not getting may strike home.
Take your meds. Lightning will be observable

in the distance. You'll admire it like an
oil by Turner.

Pale fire. Nestle the ample moon
of your husband.

Take turns being sky, orbiter.
The radio crackles Frankie's "Venus, if you will..."

then snores and picks up nothing,
electric or wry.

CHARON

Yesterday, Charon showed in a rowboat
at Mount Saint Francis Lake.

He stained the cove grey.
Years ago, I glimpsed my young parents

in a blue skiff,
fishing this lake.

They didn't look up.
The dead don't prey on us, Chuck.

We bore them, like daytime television.
Even Charon doesn't give a damn.

To make spirits speak, Odysseus
and his brave men let blood.

Doctors were so indifferent to old Mom
they didn't bother to draw any.

Here, in Indiana, the stained cork
from a 2000 Huber red pulls a nibble:

Mommy!
Omega.

Dad? He's spray, in the air
like a Fauré *Ballade*.

WITH DIGNITY

For some, hospice.
For the old cat, less.

My folks had no time to mull.
They kneeled, Mom pants down

on the bathroom floor.
Dad crashed the rug in the den.

For Jacques, dying was
a sting between his ears,

zooming out the back door,
fleeing those who petted him.

He let himself be taken
by sleet and the fox.

For him, Jacques meant dinner.
For Oakwood Funeral Home,

an easy $10,000 per Mom
or Pop in the bank.

Yet there's dignity in Yahrzeit,
the way we lift our parents

in prayer. Down the road,
wildwood rustles,

Brother Fur, Brother Fur.

LISTENING TO AM RADIO ON SATURN

Spacecraft Cassini recorded Gatling static—
    titanic thunderstorms, lightning strikes
        fiercer than hits on earth.

Everything amped. Bo Diddley revved to the skies,
    windows jacked wide in the
        Chevy. Hell, make it a T-Bird, red,

top down on Sunrise Highway,
    racing the drawbridge to working-class
        Long Beach, no cabanas, Tony and Angelo

in undershirts, hot dogs, mustard, gossip,
    sexy virgins—who was a slut?
        Hoop slips, poodle skirts,

cinch belts,
    Elvis, Conway, the Bopper,
        we breathed AM radio like

sunny cologne, like a bridge
    out of childhood, gunning it
        toward being gutted,

attack dogs, illegal abortions,
    a President's fine brain
        splattered on leather, on silk,

Cu Chi, Da Nang, Phnom Penh.
    Could we drown the deafening with
        Beatles, soften the bullet hail

with good vibrations, Tibetan gongs,
throb of galactic cosmic rays, holy,
holy, holier without our shit.

GALACTIC COSMIC RAYS

Maybe they spring from the most powerful
explosions, kicked out

of their cosmic neighborhoods.
Those that make it bump into our

atmosphere. My best friend Caren, AWOL
from Hawthorne Cedar Knolls Reformatory,

rang for help on Passover.
She'd been cringing on a roof in Queens.

"No!" Mother yelled.
Caren had blown our precious seder.

Bad Caren, tossed out of her mother's house
to make room for an Arthur-Murray Romeo.

Her mother committed her and dumped
her puppy Cha Cha, replaced them

with a baby and a dick stepfather. Caren collided
into Vic, dentist turned Staten Island pig farmer

and primal scream leader, then "The Pig" himself,
the suit who bumped her for nursing their son too long.

Where are you, my pummeled ray? Last we spoke,
you and your mother were moving to Israel.

You claimed you had forgiven her.
What of your matzo-chomping best friend?

Caren, I'll bet you survived. Call me.
Even exiled star particles need a place to light,

like ashes from campfires in the wooded lot
where the "bum" lived—we'd race past,

walk each other halfway home,
double back, Zeno be damned!

How could one of us go on alone?
We split the distance between us,

until you were cast out,
our girlhood smashed into strangelets,

the world we knew dissolved.

II.

CRIMINAL ART

YOU WEREN'T THERE

Charlie adored me.
He made me sexy.

Screwed my brains out.
No one saw.

We did it in the empty cells.
I got disciplined twice

for leaving clerical,
sneaking to cell block.

He handed me the leash and ordered me
to walk the prisoner.

He took pics.
So what?

He was God.
I wanted to keep him.

He refused to use condoms.
Now we have a son.

Why did he marry that bitch Megan?
Did you catch the snap of him and me

tanning in Rhiad? We were happy!
He didn't make me do anything.

We made a baby.
He'll come back.

ODE TO WHAT CANNOT BE PRAISED

The shackles.
The overturned slave ship, Germantown,
Kentucky, Mr. Anderson's storage barn
for human cargo. Rings bolted to
ceiling beams, for chains to pass through.
Mr. Anderson tried to hide behind vines
and scrub oak.
The elders tell us that as children
they were forbidden to go near.
Nevertheless, the beams harbor memories.
Praise wood and steel that have lasted
to spill the terrible stories.

Praise those who survived the shackles
and those that faltered.
Praise the songs they sang to find wings.
Praise what lives despite
what can't be praised,
what should be named,
slavery and its traders,
Mr. John W. Anderson,
those of us who were born
Southern and still nurse
on our terrible inheritance.

OUR MAN

"Off the record?"
   The consul leaned close
      at Klezmer Café
over beer and blinis.
   At first, I didn't grasp
      the sense.
Poetry's so far off-record
   it might
      plunge
from earth.
   "Sure,"
      I mouthed.
"It's terrible,"
   he sighed,
      "what this administration
is doing—
   the loyalty tests.
      I used to be 'their man'
in Eastern Europe.
   But now? It has never been
   this bad."
I sympathized.
   He was dashing,
      and though I'm married,
we paused in Old Europe,
   in a jewelled city
      spared by the Nazis,
sipped sparkling wine
   and for a moment
      we two might have
         fallen off

the record,
  big time,
    but then
officials rejoined us.
  When I tried to contact him
    he was gone,
disparu,
  his "away" message said
    he'd flown,
erased
  by Rove-Cheney.
    Our man
deleted
  like a dove
    by a crackshot god.

HOOKED

Luckies got there first.
Picture my father, thirteen,
two years younger than my Heather,
hanging out by his junior high.
In '33, punks ran numbers
for the Coney Island mob.
He stayed clean, unlike his *gonif* brothers.
His baby sister smoked at ten
to kill her shyness, her mother's
old fears of pogroms.

His first job, Dad wrote ad copy,
three bucks a week, gave two
to his mother who scrubbed floors.
Luckies helped to ease him through
hard days, when his father found Nat's guns
and threw them into the East River,
then his pop took off for Hollywood
with Betty Boop, his animated
invention. Ripped off. A goner.

And didn't all the GI's smoke?
Part of the winning picture.
At Maxwell Field in Montgomery, what else
could a Brooklyn kid hold onto?
When he met my plush Southern mother,
didn't she smoke too? Camels.
At twenty-five, thinking herself an old maid,
Mommy also had her poison.

They switched to filters. "Healthier,"
three packs a day.
No one said stop.

They had clues though: Aunt Marilyn's breasts,
Sam's tongue cancer.
Uncle Nat the three-time loser, four,
if you count his lungs.

When Mother had her heart attack at forty-nine,
she died and they brought her back.
She stopped cold turkey. Dad?
He chugged away, the handsome, middle-aged
engine that could. Jumped rope,
popped vitamins, a health nut
with one glitch.

I want my father back.
Let me be the mother he missed,
rip the damned thing
from his adolescent hand.
He'd be here to see his grandaughter Heather
playing vibes in the senior band, dreaming
ways to sail her cool hands to Hollywood.

"Don't blame yourself," I'd say,
at last, "I was the one
who loved you."

APOLOGY

for Lila

"Just stay nineteen," old Dr. Foxler said.
You came back to the French House,
weeping. Had politely refused him.
We had no vocabulary for what he had done.

Didn't Foxler compare you
to Shakespeare's "dark lady?"
You were "exotic," he breathed.
The only African American

at our chic college.
"Black," we said then.
Pardon, mon amie.
We wrote our blues in connecting rooms.

Summer, I asked you to be my bridesmaid.
I didn't want to marry the surgeon,
but Mother insisted this was my
chance to survive.

When I gave her my wedding party list,
Mother exclaimed, "I will not have a colored girl
in this wedding!"
She lay down crying,

claimed she was going to die.
Freshman year she'd had a heart attack
carrying my trunk up the dorm steps.
Now she held that weapon in her chest.

Someone stronger would have
called her death-bluff.
I caved. "You've been cancelled
as bridesmaid,"

I told you, and why.
You came to my wedding anyway,
flew in from Boston to Long Island
in a grey linen suit.

I send this apology thirty-five years late.
Lila, when I call you,
I'll keep trying.
"Forgive me," I'll ask.

"I have a daughter who's our age, I mean
the age we were when I betrayed you."

EVEN THIS

Blessed be even this? —Lucille Clifton

Blessed be the rumors and lies
that snap at my feet like wild dogs,
even these belonged to somebody.

Blessed be the way they grow quiet
and sleepy over time.
Blessed, the strength to ignore them.

Blessed be walls of the heart.
Blessed be a glimpse of childhood,
green shag and green walls,

blessed be leaving the house,
lingering in my mother's garden
her peonies big as a child's head

and purple pansies,
velvet faces of my childhood.
Blessed be my mother who planted them.

Blessed be the weeds on her grave
that call me back to her,
garden claws and red nails.

Blessed be the dirt and burdened
fire ants, scurrying
under cut blossoms.

CRIMINAL ART

"Pickpocketing is a criminal art form throughout Poland."
—U.S. Embassy brochure, Warsaw

Your wallet,
haiku:
Spring brings thugs

to my sleeping car.
Where's my
passport?

Police advise tourists to
crack open the train windows.
Dozing passengers have been sprayed

with chemical gas.
Do not speak English.
Whisper. You'll probably be fine.

The ice cream is excellent.
Avoid the water
like antibiotic-resistant TB.

Do not dress like an Orthodox rabbi
unless you're a Black Belt.
Thugs from the League

of Polish Families,
do not mace the Chief Rabbi
until after the Pope leaves.

It is never polite to stare at the Russian mob.
That red-lipped girl is candy.
See the guy surrounded by six Jesse Venturas?

The one with the attaché case chained
to his wrist?
He's the important man!

PASSPORT CONTROL, RIGA

> *Schraibt, idn, schraibt ("Write, Jews, write")*
> —Last words of Yiddish historian Simon Subnow,
> murdered in Riga, 12/8/1941.

The young passport officer
stuns me: "I can't let you into Latvia.
Nothing I can do."
December, 1941,
my family was shipped here by Nazis,

herded with whips
into Bikernieki
and Rumbala.
Now I can't say Kaddish
at the killing field.

His superior waves me through.
My friend the rabbi has been pacing.
"You can't predict in Riga,
It's hit or miss," our guide says.
We'll tour memorials for 70,000 Jews,

for my great-aunt Hilde Lemberger
and her son Freddie.
"What would have happened to a six-year-old?"
I asked the director of the Jewish Museum.
"They killed him." Waves his hand.

"Rumbala" means "rapids," our guide explains,
"like a river."
25,000 machine-gunned in two days.
"Faster! Faster!"
Nazis streamlined

the local fascist program,
"a definite plan to deprive
non-Latvians of the possibility
of existing."
In basements, forests,

mass graves,
German and Latvian police
carried out secret order Number One:
"The efforts of anti-Semite
circles aimed at self-purification

should not be hindered.
They should be provoked, intensified,
and directed,
in such a way that
no traces [of German orders] are left."

No traces of Jews.
As the Russian army drew closer
Kaiserwald inmates were forced
to unbury the dead at Hochwald
and burn them.

Then the diggers were shot.
Erased from camp records.
The rabbi and I have come for them,
too. We stride the city sidewalks
Jews were forbidden.

In the woods we'll chant Kaddish
for Freddie and Hilde Lemberger,
the Schwarzes from Horb,
Hilde and Max Kahn,
Jetchen Strauss,

and Wolf Kappel,
whose neighbor forced him
at gunpoint
to dig his own grave
in his own backyard.

AT BIKERNIEKI

Let not the earth cover my blood.
Let not my screams go unheard.
—Job

In this forest outside Riga
Nazis massacred 30,000.
The German War Graves Commission
has raised sculpture so ethereal you can stroll
                        through it,
paths dotted with white obelisks.
You could almost forget what happened here, winter, 1941.

Our guide says that one woman
on the tour kneeled
weeping and hugged a stone.
She studies me.
My family was on the Stuttgarter transport.

Spring breezes brush the oaks
at Bikernieki.
More than sixty years have passed.

My friend the rabbi repeats
to the stones,
"I have come to see you."

We chant the Kaddish
for our list of names
and place small stones among those

left here by mourners
pebbles—
men, women and children.

Then the road to the woods was strewn
with suitcases, prayer books,
family photos.

"The smell of burning corpses was pervasive,"
a survivor said. Now the air
is perfumed by lime trees.

Kaddish uplifts us
the rabbi explains, and adds luster
to the path of the departed.

They wanted water, hot food,
the arms of their relatives.
Not stones for pillows.

QUESTIONS AFTER THE POETRY READING

Schorr Foundation for Jewish Culture, Warsaw

"Poland is steeped
in the blood of Jews.
So, what do you think
of Poland?" The director
presses, "On my daughter's class trip
to Treblinka, kids spotted
wild strawberries. 'Later,'
their teacher promised.
After the tour they couldn't stomach
the berries.
So, what do you think?"

I stammer.
At Majdanek, our guide explained,
"There was no grass here then.
It had all been eaten."
Isaac—the little ram?

My interrogator won't swallow.
"So, what do you think
of Poland?"
Except for the hair and shoes
I think
the clover at Majdanek
grows lush
like a Monet.

Crows scream.
Families of black wings.
Monuments name "Nazi perpetrators,"
not Germans.

One headstone for a million
Jewish children
spells out "Nazi German barbarians."

So?
She dares me to translate smoke.
"I expected your words to be
more spiritual," she says.

Who can blame her
for craving music
more than heat?
Where's
balm to turn the Jewish body
invisible
as Elijah?

Touring Majdanek
I breathed grit.
"Is it real?" I asked.
Two tons of ashes domed in Soviet concrete.
"It's real," a young Jewish guide said,
pushing her son in his stroller.
"Let our fate be a warning!"
chiseled in Polish
on a gray spaceship above shards.

On our city tour of paved-over rubble,
"Warsaw Ghetto" posters
boasted prime real estate:
"Great view of *Umschlagplatz*!"
300,000 Jews were assembled here
for transports.

Our guide was worried.
Her picture had been posted on "Blood and Honor,"
an anti-Semitic web site registered in the U.S.
Her Jewish friend had been stabbed in the lung.
"Poland for the Poles!"

I think Poland is a complicated monster.
The Russian mob here eats blini and caviar.
Americans take souvenir photos
of the buffet
and of their own plates.
Americans do not often taste ashes.
At Majdanek Nazis used them
for fertilizer, landfill.

The woman asking questions
does not have to be polite.
She is the human remembering,
not a crow or bird of prey.
Song and dance will not fly here.
In a country steeped in the blood
of three million Jews,
what would it mean to be
"more spiritual"?

SLEEVE UNDER GLASS
Majdanek, Lublin

In a gallery, you'd think
chic, wearable art.

Reread:
"Fabric from Jewish hair."

The tresses above the case
can't scream.

The sleeve pitched
past human.

Blonde in demand. In Berlin,
did the commandant's wife

model this cloak
to soak up *Faustus*?

The sleeve didn't scorch her skin.
Iced champagne. Hen under glass.

The folk of Lublin who lived on the hills
overlooking the death camp,

couldn't unsee 40,000 Jews
file in from the ghetto, thousands more

from the station. In the town square,
speakers blasted Beethoven to drown screams.

Locals breathed smoke in autumn, 1942.
At the "Harvest Festival," code name *Erntfest,*

how many heads reaped
to make a pale coat?

ODE TO THE OPEN WINDOW
Sweet Briar

Like Archimedes' glass
you prove air

blue hills
scent of boxwood.

You let me glimpse
kingly cardinals

who rock the feeder
peasant sparrows

woodpeckers
on their state visit

to spring seed.
In turn they open my

childhood, hints
of my father,

gone twenty years.
I toss them cookie crumbs

and the birds bring news
of him, generous one

who left secret chocolates
and sent me Yuban

in grad school.
The feeder swings

like a scale with
the past pumping it,

Daddy weighs in
light, incorporeal,

a good man, scared man,
who loved me.

And Mom?
Not part of the bird show.

She turns up at public events,
award ceremonies,

in prize gardens,
when I'm handling money.

She watches over Heather
at Northwestern,

always craved ivy.
March, and the sash

stays open, though
when I have the chance to view

Mother in the casket,
I say: not this time.

After the funeral pageant
she had ordered fire,

though some deemed cremation
scandalous for a Jew.

Stylized,
she may have been worried

about how she would look
in her bones.

One can forgive ashes,
leave violets

by the headstone.
Sunlight and sprouting earth

prove the here-and-now
as spirits float through you.

III.

CURRENTS

TODAY THE RIVER

Today the Garonne runs greener than the poplars,
more limber, sky's smoke pierced
with light. Gulls scrawl on sheafs of cloud,
like childhood scribbles on Jones Beach.

The river's more fluid than people,
who get stuck in arguments,
in graves. Jones Beach outings all but buried,
my mother and father the ashes of driftwood.

They got stuck when their bodies
deserted, my father one year older
than I am now—what would I say to them
if they drifted past on this grassy green river?

If they made the terrible effort to come back,
my father who deserted me for his bad heart,
my mother drifting past without her burdens,
could I love them quickly enough to be grasped?

My childhood scribbles Jones Beach like a willow,
runs greener than poplars by the Garonne.

TWO JEWS

The *directrice* boasts "two Jews"
   in her house, and she wants
to share us. That's normal.
   "Looks good for her," she chirps,

to host two Jews *chez elle.*
   She tried to hook us up with
two more, further south, baffled
   when we called—to boost her image.

In deep France one finds Catholics
   and roosters, but few Jews in the
house, save us—we're boosting her.
   Further south, others remember.

In deep France, it looks good, few Jews.
   Plumped up, *la directrice* boasts two.

POOR MONSIEUR

Poor Monsieur Assen, no teeth, won't speak
about war. "Not today," he sighs,
meaning, "You'll croak before I'll spill to you."
He was "too young," he insists, to know war.

"Not today," he sighs, about the war,
meaning, "Never, brazen *Américaine!*"
He was "too young" to know
collaborators from heroes.

Never, noisy *Américaine!*
Word, he's today's source about the War.
If you want to talk collaborators,
you must buy him a bottle of Sancerre.

Claims he's too young. His wife laughs aloud.
Poor Monsieur, she loves his gums and snores.

AMIABLE

Stefane's doggie doesn't know he's French.
I like him for that—no
snippety tongue, no snobbery.
He wags his stubby tail and grins.

I like him for that. He doesn't
slobber, no kissy-kiss,
he wags, grins, ignores me,
so we can each return to business.

No kissy-kiss, no wet tongue,
unlike some important men
who wag, smile and slobber
over girls, oozing, "It's custom!"

He wags his stubby tail and grins.
Stefane's doggy doesn't know he's French.

FIG BREAD

Dark crust bejeweled
with figs, we ladies thought we'd pass out
when we slathered it with Brie.

We swooned and let go
of body image,
Weight Watchers,

swigged Sancerre
and chomped some more.
Reader, don't bother me

with your fat grams!
I devoured a loaf
smeared with homemade Brie.

Tell my husband
I've left him for crumbs.
I can never go home to Wonder Bread, Tennessee.

MUSSELS

The mussels emerged
pale as tourists who won't risk the sun

and though we politely ate them
all of us dreamed

hideous deaths on the banks of the Garonne
pirate ship agonies

bowel indignities
in this French town with no hospital.

Where would they take us?
To the salon or the *crêperie*?

We vowed to be better people
to eat less chug less Bordeaux

if only we survived the white
buttery bites of flesh

the ones from the market
in Valence d'Agens

next door to that American-loving
hunk of a cheese man.

CURRENTS

Form should never sail thoughtlessly—
   did the creatrix go on autopilot
when she shaped the Garonne?

As for the human firmament   and the nuclear plant
                  so contained
one can only spy it
   from one view.

Do not derange yourselves *Messieurs*
et Madames
   at the *concours*
      the dogs   may be cuter
                  than the persons—
   still some are badly used
   in deep France.

The short man next door screams at his
terrier   "Deek! Deek!"
               whips him   wonders
why the dog won't come
               when called.

Form should never be the master
               or the whipped dog.

Let it quicken   like the Garonne
                  don't speak
of the nuclear plant   as if
               it had roots.

This morning the grassy
green-grape ripples   swiftly

the river's cleaning itself
but the girls won't swim there.

Our tour guide confides
she yearns for Paris

leads us to the bell tower for a view
of Auvillar

diagrams of the transit of Venus
and the abandonned Garonne—

men in harness pulled the boats
upriver—donkeys watched on?

Now ships have switched to the canal.
When I ask if the Plague struck town

in the Middle Ages,
the girl cries "*Non!*" insulted.

The Germans did not linger,
headquartered in the castle

at Valence d'Agens.
She does not mention

those who were denounced here.
No plague, no *boches*

no screens
on the windows.

If you love buzzing crawling
things   a few elderly collaborators

ruines with satellite dishes
secular Catholics and underworked donkeys

chickens with heads on,
three-buck Bordeaux

this is a parfait—
espresso, glaces aux noisettes

kissy-kiss
right, left, but where

O where
are the Jews?

MONSIEUR OPENS UP

"Dr. Hirsch, *radiologue*,
was taken
to work with Mengele.
He was needed."

"His wife went to the gas.
Oui, Auschwitz."

"The Duponts hid his two children
in Auvillar."

"After the war, *le docteur*
returned, bought 15 houses,
wanted to start a Jewish colony.
A pretty town. The Jews weren't interested."

"The doctor was not a good landlord.
He fought with the mayor.
The mayor cried, 'What more do you want?
We hid two Jewish children!'"

"Now the doctor's son lives in Paris,
his daughter's in a home."
Monsieur gestures, places a heavy hand
on an invisible head.

"Her brother," he says,
"did this to her."

"The doctor was always bickering
with town officials."

Monsieur makes his hands into puppets.
The mayor, the doctor,
butt fists, again, again.

MADAME ASSEN REMEMBERS THE GI'S

"We were all saying Mass
on the day of Liberation,
when the jeeps rolled into town!"

"We spilled out, cheering!"
Madame stands, radiant.
The wrinkles fall from her face.

"One of the soldiers
offered me a ride on his jeep.
For me, it was Christmas!"

"He had short red hair.
I think his name was Eric.
He gave me his dog tags."

"I had to give them back
when he left.
How I cried!"

We are all crying now,
loving the American GI's,
the good war.

Madame cracks the spell,
"The Germans were nice to us children, too.
They played with us. We became friends."

"There was a difference between
ordinary German soldiers
and the brass." Her husband nods.

But I am thinking of the Jewish children,
the ones who had no time

to make friends.

DEEP FRANCE VS. LONG ISLAND

Not that my family was mean.
They just weren't Ricards.

Dad didn't know about the Enlightenment.
Mommy didn't open her home to outsiders,

or serve them pâté
with *rouge* martinis.   No,

every ten years Mom wrangled a reunion
on Vincent Street, wrong side of the tracks.

She loathed my father's low-class Russian kin,
peasants, she invited them.

Daddy stoked the briquettes and yelled
at his mother, my Reformed mom wrapped

Idahoes with bacon inside silver paper.
If our family argued over money,

over food, they were scared.
Grandma Anna had hidden from Cossacks in Minsk,

couldn't dodge poverty in Red Hook.
My daddy feared planes and so,

at twenty-two, the Air Force drafted him.
Mother feared public opinion.

How could they be Ricards?
Our family was united in distrust of non-Jews.

But those Ricards, so open-minded!
The matriarch Simone, source of manners,

tolerance, creamed caviar.
One must agree they're well-formed.

They enjoy their estate in Lesplanais,
the manor houses, the old bricks,

politics, education.
They admire Woody Allen.

And if my family had lived,
the Ricards would have opened their home

not just to me but to my loud-mouthed
cousins and Yiddish gran,

they would have beamed
rosy martinis into their hands,

though Uncle Sammy's habit
of pulling down his pants at parties

might have tested
even the enlightened.

After olives and vermouth,
Dad might have piped in,

"Y'a call this food?
Where's the diner?"

"Let's go grab a pot roast,
something to sink our teeth into!"

GOODBYE, DEEP FRANCE

If I wanted to drown, I'd choose
the Garonne, swift flowing, then still.
As if it swallowed something. Children
throw crusts, young women their sorrows.

The Garonne flows up-tempo, then stops,
green like Sunday's lemon olives.
Women throw their sorrows into this river.
Toss them in bundles, sink them with stones.

The Garonne flows olive green and swift.
Stops dead. All the fireworks on the banks
can't bring it back. Bundles sink with stones.
It stops as if too heavy to go on.

Young women sink their sorrows in the flow.
If I wanted to drown, I'd swallow the Garonne.

from

CIRCE, AFTER HOURS

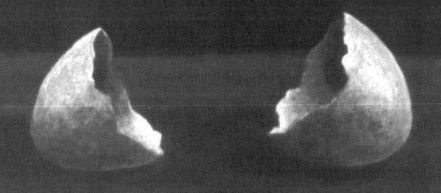

NO MAKEUP

"Makeup can only do so much,"
Marco at Bendel's said
when I went for my wedding consultation.
He would try.
To bulk up the fairy-tale aura
he glued my Turquoise and Candlelight lids
with spidery lashes.
Presto! Piled on a braided hairpiece,
a kind of hairy *challah.*

When I walked down the aisle
that first time, 1969,
the year of Zefferelli's
Romeo and Juliet,
I was a vision of loneliness.
My father, who offered
under his breath, "You don't have to
marry him!" gave me away.
I didn't get stoned until the reception
where drunk Uncle Sammy
pulled down his pants.
(It's on the video).

But what happened at the motel
was no joke. I pulled off
the hair and eyes.
Marriage!
With a man whose body
made me cringe
as if I was the ingenue
facing Fatty Arbuckle.

I couldn't hide.
Prayed for him
to fall asleep early.

Why did I marry him?
At twenty, who knew about being born?
Mother insisted I was lucky
to find someone who loved me.
"A miracle," she crooned,
"a Jewish doctor."

"I'd rather die than marry him,"
I said.
"Then die," she said.

Three years and I was ready to jump
from our Stuy Town window.

I was rescued by a cowboy
and a Jungian.
In one dream,
my mother, sister and I
wore wedding dresses in a rowboat
at sea. "There's Moby Dick!" I yelled.
"Row back to shore
for the wedding!" Mother ordered.
"You go," I said.
"I have to stay here and fight."

I left him.
The next years
made sexual history.
I'm no shaman, but I've lived and died
many times, and here I am singing.

This morning, a raccoon
looked in the mirror
after a night of writing.
"Makeup can only do
so much," I thought.
"I'll have to rely on poetry,
won't I?"
And how, at fifty, I love
nakedness
in my face and lines,
and in your hands, dear reader.

MONSIEUR MOREAU

Monsieur Moreau must be dead by now.
He was the *père de famille*
of the household where I boarded,
in 1967, Avenue du Parc Montsouris.

One evening, during the family supper,
Monsieur reminisced about the day
the Paris police arrived at the factory
where he worked, and "took away the Jews."

"Les juifs." He giggled. I
swallowed, the leek soup, an onion.
In her black dress,
Madame looked even more like a crow.

They were hard workers,
la bourgeoisie,
solid, Monsieur and Madame.
Both of them must be dead by now.

Paris is beautiful, no question.
Et oui, vive la Résistance!
Paris hated the Nazis, *les boches.*
At the auto plant, no one hid Jews.

Beneath his little clownlike mustache,
Monsieur giggled.
No question.
Perhaps he died in his bed, quietly,

on the *belle* Avenue du Parc Montsouris.

THE HEDGEHOG

Sheila says, "The little hedgehog lives
in the shade of the mulberry tree."
I'm back at Madame's table, 1967.
She's serving unchewable grey meat.

In my best student French
I offer, *"C'est délicieux, Madame,
mais, qu'est-ce que c'est?"*
("Great stuff—what is it?")

"C'est du hérisson."
The word shuddered.
After supper, I rushed
to my Larousse—

"hedgehog"! Next day
I queried my French friends,
"Is it a delicacy?"
"Mais non!"

Madame, by now you cook no more.
But the hedgehog lives on.
Your crimes were small, mostly
committed at table.

I'm told you served
petit âne for Christmas, a sweet
little ass from Montmartre. Alas,
I left Paris before the festivities.

Did Monsieur help you carve?
"Tais-toi, tu m'embêtes!"

you'd yell at him, stunned beast,
each night after soup.

Might I mention dessert, the night
you handed us boarders a bowl of lemons
urging, *"Prenez! Prenez!"*
You insisted that we each eat one.

I paid you back, didn't I,
murdering your language
each time I opened my hungry
Yankee mouth.

TROUT

Beau is babbling about German phone sex,
a pro on the cover of some slick highbrow mag
mouthing "Give it to me!"
in her gutteral tongue.

My phone sex in German
would be short.
I recall only the ditty
about the irritable trout:

Ziemlich schlecht,
sagt der Hecht,
in der Tiefe
Liebesbriefe.

Bad news,
said the sea trout,
in his love letter
from the deep.

Bad news is not what customers
pay to hear.
Bad news, all I remember from that summer
with the Nazi at Columbia,
German 101, drinking songs at 8 a.m.,
hoisting *du, du* ... alone
in the language lab.

Beau and I struggle
with two different languages.
He speaks twenty-year-old WASP on his way
to the regatta,
the rap of a beautiful man

on his way to any woman he damn well chooses.
I talk fifty-year-old wife and mother,
Jewish teacher, for whom German jokes don't
come easy.

Jews don't sail,
I want to tell him,
We put an ocean between us and the Cossacks.
Kept our feet on city sidewalks after that.
But for Beau I might put on a life jacket.
I might take summer lessons like an
underprivileged trout.

I'd let him teach me waves,
call him Captain,
O, Captain.

"No! You wouldn't seriously
consider it?"
my old friend Bill exclaimed.
"That would be grotesque."

At forty-five, Bill himself
had a fling with Jan
the teenaged painter
who gave phone sex to pay her rent.
Jan was something of a sailor.
She could only come underwater.
For Bill, that was a summer
of Great Lakes.

Great art is grotesque, no?
Think of Picasso.
Think of anything but a young man
with his looks and his poetry
his music and his crooning
his painting and his and his
mouth-watering
trout.

NO SALE

How would a Jewish girl
sell her soul to the Devil?
Reformed don't believe
in Beelzebubba.

Now Robert Johnson, he
had no such trouble.
You know the tale, how the bluesman
sold his soul at the crossroads

for a lifetime of hot-lick guitar.
Shot by a jealous husband
at the roadhouse, he died on his knees,
they say, drunk, barking like a dog.

Odd, for a nice Jewish girl
to fall on her knees.
Years though, that's how
it was. Me shot down,

baying at the moon
for a lick of you.

CIRCE, DID YOU?

Circe, like those siren sisters you warned of,
did you croon men to your shore?
Did you surround-sound sailors with silky hair
and nipples? *Oooh,* when you stroked them
with syllables, did it matter to your tongue
who they were? Or were you waiting for one,
Odysseus, with his many-skilled fingers?
In the ruby-tipped dawn did you hold out
for the master mariner, craving mutual song?
Had you dreamed his lure of black hair,
called out his snake-charmer's name, long after
you had previewed that shaggy dog ending?

Sometimes names trick us into dreams
of having. Odysseus,
an undercurrent, a squall.
Hurricane Odysseus.
Circe, blown away.

IT CAN'T HAPPEN

Not now not ever
not at your house, your living room,
your couch, not in the late afternoon
not while my husband's waiting
my daughter's on hold
not at my house not in the hot tub
not with wine, coke, or dope
not with Mexican, Colombian, hydrotropic, not
now.

Not in my office
on my desk
not in the meadow under stars
not with whiskey or Ecstasy
not in this lifetime not now.

Not unless
you fall down on your knees
not unless you cry, beg, bleed,
not unless our lips brush
not unless your caress blots out memory
not unless you're bigger than your myth
not unless you've grown braver
not unless your hair's still curly
not unless you write a poem for me
and slam it hard enough to kill reverie
not unless you call me
write to me
not now not ever not unless.

JEALOUS

Mount Saint Francis Lake

I'm jealous of those parents.
Their goslings gliding in a line
between stately Mom and Dad
don't suddenly turn and announce
"I want to go to Interlochen!"

Goslings don't yearn to play
marimba. They don't fly
to snowy Michigan and leave
bereft parents in Knoxville.

It won't cost the farm
to send them to gliding
and honking school.
Alone, their mother and father
won't suddenly turn
to one another and think
"What now?"

After their kids go
these two will sail
the cool water,
shit on the dock,
eat bugs.
The lake buoying them
will remind them
of their own mother,
her unflappable calm, her
noisy temper flaring
when foxes crept
or humans stomped down to the edge.

Their wings will recall ancestral
flight patterns.
There will be no nostalgia,
no twinges in the feathers,
no grabbing ankles and pulling down.

BODILY HARM

When Libby's twenty pound boa
struck at the rat, I dropped my tea
on her snowy carpet.

Long as a squirrel, the white rat
had been frozen.
Libby's husband reheated it
in the microwave (where I had been
thinking of warming my tea).

Boa embraced her rat dreamily.
If you didn't know
she was choking what she
thought was a live one,
you would have guessed she adored him.

I warmed to them.
She reminded me of Tom
from Utica, that all-too-tight
embrace, how I'd have to explain
when he caught me talking to a man.
To be fair, we took turns strangling,
being rats.

So that when he came after me,
when the New York State police
rang me with "We don't want to
alarm you, but..."
I was scared, but not stunned.

Luckily he stopped himself
en route with a butcher knife.
Married now, him to a

nurse from Brooklyn, me
to a regular Joe
who doesn't lunge at pets,
we've both got all the hugging
we can swallow.

THE HIT

In Brooklyn there must have been no lawn
and little bread, so when we made it

to Long Island, Daddy fed the birds.
"No, no, no!" he'd cry, if I threw crusts.

"You have to tear the pieces into crumbs."
He pretended not to know the Mob.

When the don invited him to Atlantic City
with the "Family," Daddy replied,

"I'll have to see if my wife has plans."
Good for a laugh. Clean,

Dad lent cover.
Before they threatened him.

"Pull your vending machines out of that bar,
or we'll kill your wife and children!"

their goon growled on the phone.
"No!" Daddy said. So they sent a guy

disguised as the gas man
to grab me and my sister.

Wiretaps caught the hit
before they whacked us.

Daddy made a cleancut witness.
A shame he never got the chance to vote.

Did I mention that he was a felon?
He was framed.

Just a businessman.
Good-looking hustler, no crook.

In '66, Senator Javits
secured a pardon for my Dad.

Bobby Kennedy would have signed it, too,
but someone sent a guy after him.

Daddy died anyway from smoking Lucky Strikes.
Dark-haired, like me,

he was the one who named me "Marilyn."
We hardly ever saw him.

After late-night stops in Brooklyn
he'd leave chocolate jelly rings

in our "Good Fairy Bowl."
Mornings when I feed the birds

I'm his daughter again, scattering crumbs
like secrets, or ashes.

GLOBAL

Mother would have loved global warming.
A good Alabama girl, she resented
cold Long Island mornings
and my Brooklyn-born father,
who had dragged her North, toward snow.

She'd phone me long distance at college,
in those days a hefty bill, her voice
all tremolos: "The paper's calling for sleet
in Boston! Aren't you freezing?
Be careful!" October through April.

Even in her mink stole Cecelia grew cold,
colder, when Daddy's sister Marilyn
lay dying of cancer. Leaning
over her, Mother spat out,
"You brought this on yourself!"

"Now I have to drive all the way
from Long Island to Rockaway.
So much trouble because of you!"
Aunt Marilyn, thirty-three,
too sick to cry.

After Daddy died, Mother grabbed the urn,
headed south like a migratory bird,
rejoined her Montgomery girlfriends,
most of them widows by then.
She tended her roses and hibiscus.

But she couldn't escape having lived
in New York. No longer at ease

paying "the girl" eight bucks a day,
she upped the ante to thirteen, a scandal.
White-haired in the New South, was she warming?

When Mother grew tired of ashes,
she up and buried Dad, without the mourner's
Kaddish. She had loved him like fire.
Then she dumped him. Cold act,
something a poet or dictator might do.

Yet Mother was afraid of frost,
of losing her mother's lap,
her sunny toddler's lawn on Le Braun Avenue,
her native tongue of slow syllables.
There was a dry, icy spot

inside her, and if she wasn't careful
(she rarely was), it would burn
her stylized planet, freeze her motherhood
and Brownie Scouts, forty years of Sunday School,
teaching at the Home for the Blind,

ice down the tenderness my grandma had left her—
Grandma planted next to Daddy's urn
in Montgomery's Oakwood, not far
from poor Hank Williams, so lonesome he could die,
over in the restricted Christian section.

THE LADIES

When Daddy had sold enough used cars,
my Southern mother bought a metal washtub,
stuck it in the basement
of our Long Island home
for the live-in maid to bathe in.
No way "the girl" could use our bath!
Just up from Alabama, the teenager sobbed
behind the door of her room.
Mommy said she cried too much,
we had to send her back.

Twelve years later,
Micky Schwerner, a Jewish college student
raised on Long Island, like me,
was murdered by the Klan in Mississippi.
I told myself *now my mother will*
understand the struggle.

"He asked for it!" she snapped.
"Should have stayed in New York
where he belonged."

Not until she was eighty, back
in Montgomery, did Mother join a protest
to restore public transportation
to the inner city.
And when a young black man—her escort
to the rally—drove up to her plush apartment,
the snowy-haired neighbors watched
with horror from behind their drapes.
Being good Southern ladies,
no one said a thing.

FINALLY

Finally (one year down) I dreamed my mother
was dead, no, that she was dying.
"My heart has closed," she explained.
This time I was with her,
in the crowded atrium of a school.
This time I helped her to lie down,
ran to find a pillow, but by the time
I came back she was gone,
just a blanket on the floor.

So I chatted with schoolgirls
about pocketbooks—their large, sumptuous
leather bags, their fabulous matching luggage.
"If you can't afford what I have,
then you're not a good role model,"
one attractive young woman said.

...

Maybe it wasn't the medication
that killed her,
or the smug inattentive specialist.
Her heart had been closed to me
for a long time, but she was alive,
wasn't she, she loved my sister,
and my daughter, and I could watch her loving.

I had just been with her for Mother's Day,
driven the long hours to Montgomery.
I was a good daughter, wasn't I?
She was woozy and scared.
The young temp doctor had changed her

heart pills and suddenly she could
feel the beat jumping wildly
and no one would listen.

"What would happen if you didn't go home
right away?" Mother pleaded.
"I have to turn in my grades," I said.
"Oh," she sighed.

Next day the call reached me at home.
How they found her on the bathroom floor.
No Southern Lady would have smiled on this.

No daughters.
No blanket and no pillow.

And the luggage? I went on a leather-
buying binge after the ashes.
Credit kept me covered.
Department stores gave me hope.
I could be anyone.
Wasn't I an American?
With the tote bags and satchels
couldn't I carry myself? Why
did I need a mother?

Well stuff my mouth,
as they used to say down home.
Why shouldn't I stuff my closet
with sleek hides instead of howling?

HORB

City etched in glass
at the Holocaust Museum.
Your name offers the roundness
of a planet,

curves of an hourglass
running out.
Your name still beautiful
though your Jews were herded off.

Horb, centuries, a moment,
no more. Out of a hundred Jews,
forty could not emigrate.
Easy to track in 1939

after the German minority census.
Sofie Sara Schwarz.
Berta Sara Schwarz.
The humiliation of "Sara"

added to each Jewish woman's
name according to racial law.
Louis Israel Schwarz
Rubin Israel Schwarz.

My uncles stamped.
"The Nazi regime emulated
segregation laws then current
in the U.S."

In the beginning there were benches
and bathrooms: "Jews Only!"
All this frenzied purity and Horb
restricted its country air.

The forest did not disappear.
At its heart, the Jewish cemetery stands,
the stones of earlier generations overgrown:
Ernestine, Isak, Liebmann, Lina...

SURVIVOR

The Night of Broken Glass,
thugs set fire to the Rexingen synagogue.
Scorched the Torah.
Officials blamed "outsiders."
Or kindergartners playing with matches.
Jews on the fire brigade who doused the flames
were taken to Dachau.

Beginning of the end of three centuries
of Jewish life in Rexingen, Mühringen, Horb.
Sixty emigrated.
Ten "died on the spot."
Others were doomed to Theresienstadt,
Auschwitz, Riga.
After 1942, only one of the Schwarzes
from Horb survived deportation.

Hedwig had seen too much.
She died in Marienhospital,
Stuttgart, 1952,
fifty miles from her birthplace.
What held her to the land
of shards and ashes?

Was she lured by the
old cemetery, resting place
of her parents and grandparents?
Was the call of the dead more powerful
than *Shavei Zion*?
Perhaps the leaning firs
of the Black Forest reminded her
of her girlhood, her mother.

Nothing romantic about Terezín.
The ghetto taught her to decipher
tales of witches, children lured
to ovens. A few prisoners
had returned from Auschwitz,
told the truth about "the East."
No gingerbread houses.

But the Red Cross believed
in fairy tales.
For them, Theresienstadt
was a spa, overflowing with *Brundibár,*
soccer matches, cheerful kids.
After the official visits,
the children were transported to
Auschwitz-Birkenau.

The health care and retirement
package the Nazis had promised
turned out to be typhus, spotted fever,
starvation.

On Sunday, in hospital,
the Sisters of Saint Vincent de Paul
might have wheeled her out for a stroll.
Silence was good medicine,
they thought.

No words to ward off nightfall.
The dead were never far.

TO MY POEM OF HOPE

I don't blame you for hope,
for wanting the children
to have survived.
Because their names were not
inscribed in the "minority registration,"
you assumed they had slipped
through the net.
My dear, Horb was a hillbilly dot.
Everyone knew everyone.

Now we find this handwritten entry
by Hedwig Schwarz
in her daily book of prayer:
"On Friday, November 28, 1941
at 5:50 AM, our dear good daughter
Hilde Sara Lemberger and our dear
good grandson Siegfried Israel Lemberger
moved away from here.
We only wish that God may watch over them
and that they stay well."

Their grandmother kept "Sara" and "Israel"
in case of Nazi eyes.
Mother and son "moved away from here"
in early darkness.
The rooster couldn't crow.

The files reveal that Hilda
and Siegfried, called "Friederle"
were deported "east for labor assignment,"
"that is to say, Riga,"
"declared dead on 1/4/1942."

Für tot erklärt.
Pronounced by anonymous agents
with past participles on their hands.

Dear poem, if we look again,
and we must,
we will find scraps,
scrawled words, secret histories,
the cry between the lines:
"Remember. They called me Freddie.
I was six years old.
Here's what really happened."

MEZUZAH

In Memory, Hedwig Schwarz

In the doorpost of her house, a hollow
where the *mezuzah* used to hang.
I press my hand against the indentation,
my way of speaking to the past.

Touch the hollow where the *mezuzah*
used to hang. In Horb, Nazis renamed her street
Hitlerstrasse. My way of speaking to the past
is to listen, press the old men for answers.

1941, Jews were packed into *Hitlerstrasse.*
Now it's a winding picture-postcard road,
Jew-free, pleasant as it seemed
before Nazis pressed my family into *Judenhausen.*

I press my hand against the indentation.
Over Horb, a hundred doorposts echo, hollow.

from

How to Get Heat
Without Fire

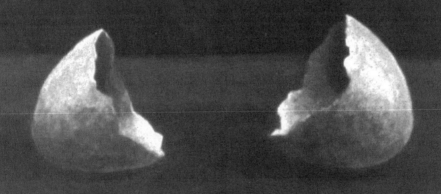

FORGET THE SILK

Forget the silk of poppies, their unrelenting red, I could
take you to forgetting, lick amnesia across your lashes,
make you forget half-learned love, forget your name
and the word for blood, caress you with my breasts until you
spill your hair over me and we're lost in a silkstorm.
Forget the drained desert stars. Hold me fast as constellations
you painted on your ceiling as a boy, unfold me like a true
    map,
wander my sleepless byways. Taste the dark-skinned girl
you used to love coming toward you without sorrow.
Surprise the man you mourned hiding blues inside
his hair—we'd be the bridge drumming one world
into another, riding our breaths. Over, under, all around,
crooning our own night chant, fingering cries.
Could you bear forgetting this?

SAYING GOODBYE

We embraced, there in the parking lot
of the ordinary.
How could I know your arms were arguing last things?
Your cheek in my hair.
For a moment, I pressed against you. Goodbyes can be vast.
In a breath, we traded lives. I didn't know you
were a cliff I had reached the edge of.
Your touch echoed.
I simply followed it like song.

WHY I WEAR MY HAIR LONG

I want to wrap it
around you
like a silk shirt

button it
slowly
carefully,

facing you
let the fringes
tickle your hips

until we ride
strong silken horses
glued on

& my flag
unfurls
a few strands

sticking
to your
lips.

BAD SEX

There's no such thing as bad whiskey or bad sex.
—Roland Flint, quoting a friend in L.A.

We were screamers that year.
Gina, the lady downstairs told me
when we woke her and her truckdriving boyfriend,
she'd get angry with *him* about our shaking the house—
"Why can't you do that for me?"

1970, a year Reich would have envied.
Beethoven's Ninth in sex, loud, deaf to others.
Mike, the nineteen-year-old cowboy from Teaneck,
me, twenty-five.
Nights he didn't come five times he felt
pent up. For me
it was the beginning of life in the body,
genesis, exodus from a dry marriage,
numbers and revelations.

Once, in a New Brunswick flophouse,
high noon, we sweated so hard the soaked sheets
slid off the plastic-covered
mattress and so did we. Wetness and the smell of sex
permeated the year like a rain forest.

How did it end? Tired.
In a frenzy of suspicion I read his diary—
I knew it! He'd cheated on me
with a woman from his office. She wore red gloves
he wrote, he came five times.

Now I'm older stats aren't the key.
Yet I hold to 1970, sex so good
my whole body and the next life and the next,
pre-reincarnated, came.
Even today I wear red gloves
as a tribute to that unknown woman
who took the next shift
and as a way of saying, thank you, Mike.

THE DREAM

After nights of Lamaze and days
of layette sets,
I dream the dam breaks:
from back down the road
waters and rocks
rush toward me. I'm savvy,
having seen *Tidal Wave*
on TV, I run for high ground.
My belly and swollen feet slow
me down, though I escape into
Falwell's skyscraper, where
Jerry himself comforts me.
Distinguished, silvery-haired,
God holds my hand. When I wake up
the true disaster dawns on me:
I have been saved
despite being a Long Island Jew.
The dam I understand, but this?
As I fold the baby's clothes
I realize of course
I want to be born again,
to be fed, hugged, loved,
changed, and changed, and changed!

LOVERS

Heather's hands are all over me like a lover's.
"Mama, Mama," she croons, loving the sounds.
Locked into each other's eyes, both of us laughing.
She smells so sweet, her skin's like vanilla.

"Mama, Mama," she croons, "*mmm...*"
After breakfast her pajamas smell like maple sugar.
She smells so sweet, her skin's talcum and vanilla.
"Mama," she asks, "may I smell your nipple?"

Her pajamas smell like maple sugar.
I'm surprised, but "Sure, Honey, how does it smell?"
"Mama, Mama, *mmm...*"
"It smells wonderful, Mama!"

Locked into each other's eyes, laughing together,
Heather's hands are all over me like a lover's.

UNUSUAL

I.

Cold white sun. Pam's off at the sperm bank
checking "Anglo-Saxon."
A wary shopper, she passed on the box marked
                                    "unusual."
How sick I am of categories!
Do the trees care that the sky has no roots?
Pines and sky interplay, windy winter blues.
Why not say "breath" for sky and branches?
Why call me "slow" when I may be racing toward
                                    another life?
Oh, I can see myself in your rear-view mirror,
plucky like a sperm on my way to the bank,
determined, it's pay day,
breathe, breathe, wiggle wiggle, I'm an unusual
                                    metaphor,
Reeboks instead of flagella.

Pam calls back—she's learned that "unusual"
means Native American.
It's 1941, Berlin, and I'm
unusual, hell, we're all a heartbeat away
from unusual. We all love our children past
categories, we'd invent any subterfuge to save them,
give them our breath, swallow this white sun,
dragons breathing fire on the Klan, a belch
                                    for that boy
in Heather's class who said the Jews were stupid,
better save a candleflame for Mrs. English
so she'll recant the narrow outline,
reteach the whole Fourth Grade—
                        this time that writing outside
the margin

is lovely, the practice of wind and trees and sun,
unusual grandmothers and grandfathers
praying for the shining mothers and fathers
on our way to God-knows-where.

2.

In bed, when I tell him about my sperm-walk,
my concern about suddenly seizing the *macho*—
do I secretly want to be a man?
Lou says, "There's a big difference between
being a sperm and being a man."
"What's the difference?"
"A man is alive, a sperm, debatable."
"And sperm don't know where they're going,"
I add. "Neither do most men,"
says Lou.

THE GENIUS TEST, FIRST GRADE

Miss Howe let the lady take me
down to the basement
where we used to huddle for bomb drills.
"You were chosen for this test," she said.
"In your own words, tell me what this means:
An ill wind blows nobody good."

I was Miss Howe's pet, her
best reader, I loved her,
and I could feel the sick wind filling me,
but I couldn't make my body speak
through my brain to this grim stranger.
My ordinariness hung over us,
blanketing our lungs and pores.
A failure at five. A dumb little fish.
She threw me back upstairs.

I didn't know it then
but in 1951 things were going badly
for artists in America
and things were about to get worse.
"President Eisenhower is eating bombs
for breakfast," *Life* would report.
Pediatrician Dr. William Carlos Williams
would never sit in his Poetry Office
at the Library of Congress, not
while paranoid fallout cloaked the House.

"Be quiet and put your heads down!"
Mr. Stone, our principal, walked
        the stuccoed corridors,
a finger pressed to his lips.
When the town sirens blew

no one bothered to tell us
at Oceanside School Number Five
whether or not it was for real.

I planned on running home.
If I was going to die,
I wanted to be with my mother.
If it was the end of the world,
    why keep still?

Not until years later did I hear:
It's
    an ill wind
        that blows nobody good.
Senator McCarthy's black-and-white face
glaring in her living room
must have scared even the Testing Lady.
1951, we were huddled together,
there was no room for ambiguity
in a good American mouth.

BEFORE THE DISCOVERY OF THE MIND

In his *Discovery of the Mind*
Bruno Snell traces the
birth of thought to Euripides,
arguing that there can be no
"mind" without a language
for reflection. Odysseus
was mindless, Athena on his shoulder
directed traffic for what
passed as ideas.

Wake up, Bruno!
Wasn't it that pooch Argus
who had the only memory
worth a damn? And don't thinking men
sometimes lack even an organic
concept of the body?

What do you yourself remember
about the woman who held you,
crooned to you, lifted you
from hunger to her breast?

And what of the night she
didn't come when you cried?
What sounds did the dark suck back in?
Did the little nightlight help you
with its domesticated face?

When they took that light
what stirred at the end of your bed?
To test your room you hurled the
picturebook near your pillow.

What did fright say
when the book hit something where
air should have been?

When she moved toward you
you could grasp—not her face,
but terror, her
shadowy body. Your own body
awakened like a mind.

When you tried to scream
it was one of those dreams
women have, sounds won't
form in the straining throat.

Many things have no language
for fear or reflection—the moon
in black, the witch who emerges
from the bedstead. In the shift from
the unknown to *God no,* there's a
lifetime of wiring the
moving dark to words.

If I could hold you, Bruno,
we could watch for
your terror, sing to her,
woo her,

> *Mama, don't hurt me,*
> *Don't hate me or bite me.*

In my own bad dream
she was already a tiger with
her mouth open wide,

and the best I could do then
was be curious—
put my head in her mouth
(okay, it was dangerous,
but it was a way of going back in),
enter the circus performer's
fear of the trained beast.

Each time I stay longer
inside its breath,
less afraid of my own devouring.

PASSOVER

My father heads our table,
cheeks flushed from the first cup of wine.
At sunset he left his wallet upstairs
with bags of quarters from the vending machines.
He's making jokes and laughing with his mouth shut,
giving us his bright side—boy, clown, inventor.
Tonight by candlelight even the sullen teenagers
are cheerful, my sister Elaine and I,
glowing from apples and walnuts soaked in wine.
Aunt Marilyn is alive, sitting across from me.
Her breasts are hers again, untouched by cancer.
The New York Grandma is beside her
in a cotton housedress, two lines of berry lipstick
pressed on her faded mouth.
She's laughing, "*Oy*, stop it, Harry!" as my father
teases her. Letting go of want and pogroms.
My mother is no longer a martyr.
Pharoah has set her free so she can recline,
tasting her frothy matzoh balls,
delighting in all she has created.
This is Passover, an invitation
to our freer selves to join us,
an invitation to the poor to come and dine.

My father loved kids, especially poor ones,
seeing himself starving back in Brooklyn.
He liked to buy ice cream for any hungry child
he found hanging around the stand.
The prayer book tells us, "The dead shall live on earth
in the good deeds they performed here,

and in the memory of those who live after them."
That's it, no big party, though this evening
circulating like sad music in the fragrant air
all the Jews who ever lived are still alive.

EASY LISTENING MUSIC, I-75

My father liked "easy listening
music"—everything else had been hard,
Work was his birthright.
His mother Anna scrubbed floors,
carrying her youngest, Harry.
His older brothers had opted out—
a small-time crook, a big shot
with Murder Incorporated. No wonder
my father was neat—no grime,
he was proud of his fingernails,
clean little moons over clean hands.

Why do I gather clutter?
Here she is, my Grandma Anna,
standing in the narrow aisle
of her second-hand store.
Anna, saver of old sweaters, mothballs,
pogroms hidden under mounds of cloth.
She hid her guitar on top of the hall closet.
We kids would have been embarrassed
to hear her sing Yiddish,
eager as my mother was to rise
to middle-class brightness.

What songs did my grandmother
take with her from Russia?
At fifteen, did she sing her mother's
lullabies in the ship's hold?
Croon them again to little Harry,
to Nat, and Sammy, and my frightened
                           Aunt Marilyn?
Were there other babies who didn't survive
hungry nights in Coney Island?

Markers for Indian mounds slip by,
this ground I ride easily over.

The Jewish graves are dispersed,
of Anna I have
no traces—only me.
I want to be a song my grandmother
would have recognized.

Rest a little, Harry.
Sleep, my little Anna,
Shayn viday-la vo-na,
pretty as the moon.

THE POCKETBOOK

"Fluid Italian suede
in garnet,"
the copy croons.
I memorize
the Bergdorf Goodman
catalogue,
the blonde with garnet lips
carrying my pocketbook
against her slim hip.
570 dollars.
One chunk of my daughter's
college.

After weeks of foreplay
I sell out my family,
dial the toll-free number.
It's miraculously
easy, just "ten working days"
and here it is, nestled
in a silk carrying case.
For days I hide it
behind the recliner,
playing *peekaboo,*
trying it out when my husband's
not home.

Nothing else in my life's
this beautiful.
To keep it
I would have to buy
silk suits, tweed coats,
a silver Porsche,
house on Park Avenue.

My shoulders are unworthy
of the strap
in wine-red suede,
I would have to have inches
surgically added to my height.

"American women carry
their souls
in their pocketbooks,"
Edgar Allen Poe said.
Not just my soul,
my money,
my identity,
my credit cards.

This pocketbook soft
and red
like a womb,
room where I could
carry myself in comfort,
be my own mother,
be drunk with color,
570 dollars.

I could sell my
wedding ring,
break into neighbors'
houses,
after two years
in the women's
correctional facility
there it would be

waiting for me,
fluid Italian suede
in garnet,
big enough to carry
the collected works of Poe,
O my fair sister, O my soul.

DEAR ORPHEUS

Don't look
back this time,
ok, babe?
It gets wearing,
the shrieking
the tearing of limbs
stupid Furies
imitating
earthbound hacks.
Not to mention
the commute,
hell
& back
more predictable
than Amtrak.

Don't think
I'm not grateful
for these
forays,
it's just
I'm getting older
(what hell *is*, darling)
nothing new
to wear,
basic black's dowdy,
overdone.

At least let me
go first.
I'll know
better than to
glance back

when you call—
but oh! those dangling
Gala apples
big as tires
in your vowels.
Boys in sunglasses
and warm leather
the syllables
of my name
sips of *ouzo*
from your mouth...

So what if I blow it
I've been
torn to pieces
by love before
my arms know how to swim
my head knows how to sing
and I
don't mind
waking up
in fragments.

It's your turn
to silently biodegrade
into a sea
of boring
mist.

I'll
myth you.

FIREFLIES

In the dry summer field at nightfall,
fireflies rise like sparks.
Imagine the presence of ghosts
flickering, the ghosts of young friends,
your father nearest in the distance.
This time they carry no sorrow,
no remorse, their presence is so light.
Childhood comes to you,
memories of your street in lamplight,
holding those last moments before bed,
capturing lightning-bugs,
with a blossom of the hand
letting them go. Lightness returns,
an airy motion over the ground
you remember from Ring Around the Rosie.
If you stay, the fireflies become fireflies
again, not part of your stories,
as unaware of you as sleep, being
beautiful and quiet all around you.

BLACK BEAN SOUP

Black bean soup, and my mother's nineteen again.
A *whirr* of fans—it's summer in Havana.
Three women share a huge, tiled room overlooking
the Prado. "That was fifty years ago."

In Battista's Cuba, the best time of her life.
"Men handed us chocolates and flowers
as we strolled the Prado.
The chocolates had liqueurs in them."

"They loved Americans then."
Young men from New Orleans whirled them
to nightclubs. Even the chocolates were loaded.
"I didn't want to go home. Nothing for me

in Montgomery." In Havana she waltzed all night.
"Next summer I sailed the *Marguerita* to Colombia.
The President of Panama's son took me dancing.
'Rodriguez Parras,'" she rolls the *r's* on her tongue.

"We met on the boat to Baranquilla.
Our guide asked, 'Do the ladies want to see
a whorehouse?' The girls wore kimonos in the afternoon,
red carnations in their window-boxes."

"They gathered around to say hello.
I don't know, maybe they were paid to be polite.
Potted red carnations in their back windows.
It was just another profession."

"Like being a secretary, treated well in town.
Once we walked through Cienaga in our bathing suits,

the *policia* in back of us.
Why we were arrested? *'No hablo Español!'"*

"They threw us in jail.
I was wearing a white terrycloth cape.
Indecent exposure! The chief spoke English.
He let us go just in time for our boat."

"Rodriguez Parras."
She rolls the *r's* luxuriously over her tongue.
Three women look out on the Prado.
Black bean soup, and my mother's nineteen again.

IN THE FACE OF SOLITUDE

I keep my body here, with me,
reaching out to the still air,
trying to smash the stillness out,
tearing the air's silk
to find out what's beating there.

Stripped to the voice,
who will I be
in the face of solitude?
I am frightened by my skin
that cannot escape.

What is denied to love:
"a fin in a waste of waters,"
the pen in its wake.
The sky goes so slowly,
& the body goes fast.

HOW TO GET HEAT WITHOUT FIRE

Beneath the dark floor
there has always been love,
but the trick is
how to get down to it?
Shall I tear my way down
like a tiger clawing
the floorboards, when this
tearing down is what scarred you?
Whose mother is there
in the dark trying hard
to hide you from the memory
of the floorboards in flame?
How to get heat without fire?
To coax light open?
To ease you new into
the world if I am not
a mother, or a beloved?
Pull back? Peel back dead
bark, pull back the boards
we trample, throw each other
down on and through some days?
Turn the floor into a pool
we can dive deep into,
cradle the mothers,
let the animals swim their ways?
Has music ever saved anyone?
Then I will reenter my life
as sound,
as notes strung like pearls
that you have yearned
to enter.
I will be sound,

I will be sound,
and silence,
listening.

EARLY POEMS

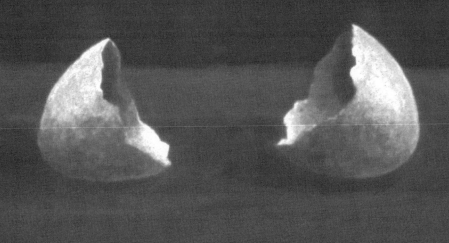

THIRST

I long for what disturbs
her, for the splinter
she complains of.
I'm jealous of what
has gotten into her today.

Nothing strikes close.

OUT

Out of order
and we know it,
the body's been left behind
without a scream.

The world wavers in front of us,
all the bright white houses waver,
as if seen through smoke or water,
our eyes are unsure.

Soft, this is all we have,
grandmothers and wolves,
our eyes to see the bigger with,
our mouths, the better, at least,
to say *no* with.

But if, after so many mouths
our words are shot in back
of the tongue,

if, after so many cries,
our silence also comes to waste us?

LIMITATION

The night before his duel, Galois
pushed the field of mathematics ahead
twenty years.

The night before his death, at twenty-one,
Galois revolutionized
field theory.

His mind bloody on the field,
his name like cigarettes,

Galois had proved that in a field
of sixteen squares,
certain permutations
are impossible.

COME

The lake is still tonight,
the rose grows grey.

Come and cull the blossom
with your tongue.

We could climb like roses.

IN THE GREAT NIGHT

In the great night
my heart will go out
in the not so great night
like this one
fears go along for the ride
in the great night
that threatens all our poetry
that tears at the body
chained to words.

Give us this dance
our daily trance

our dreams do not forget us
they spread us out like fans

& flirt over the edges
ghosts tear at the air to tell us

in the great night
self-hate will go out
like the first ball of the season
officially open   to the heart's demands.

ANNE SEXTON

Death was no rumor.
"My poems know more than I do," you said.
Your words walk ahead in the desert
carrying men on their backs.
The black sea that parts for poems,
closes down on you.

THE BLACK CLOCK BY THE SEA

Not the genius of his sea,
she sings from the shores of her skin.
The memory of him shatters
her still-life studies.
He awakened the sea in her,
not the mask of the sea.
His beauty rained hard, seed
stirred salt in her blood,
and she stayed open like an anemone.
Now the sea lies packaged,
unfurled only in dreams.
The still-life returns,
a black clock by the sea.
She waits for herself now,
the waves crest without her.
Small and beautiful,
solitude picks her like a shell.

WHITMAN'S WILD CHILDREN

Where are Whitman's wild children,
where the great voice speaking out
with a sense of sweetness & sublimity?
—Lawrence Ferlinghetti

& where would a woman learn to be wild?
Dead in first grade,
quiet legs crossed,
or stunned in bridal pictures?
What woman is a child of Walt Whitman?
Who could afford the flow?
With sharks out
there's no extra blood
for sublimity.
It's one thing, Larry,
to say come out of the closet,
but you won't get sweetness and light.

A ROOM OF MY OWN

From here the landscape of love hums
like a Mondrian roadmap.
The window overlooks the city of senses,
lights the base of the spine.
The city is wine,
"she is coming, my dove, my dear," on streetcars,
footsteps on Vallejo Street, eyes
on the Golden Gate, throat of steel.
My life, my fate, she is near.

VAMPIRE

You bled me for images
to feed your image.
I have been your poem so long
I lost my own songs.
You don't die easy
at your castle of approval.
No longer will I stand in the doorway,
a high-class hooker of words.
I break your hold on my blood.
Let the poetry go shrieking.
You won't have my death
for your imagery.

BEING MEAN TO A MYTH

Persephone's pomegranate
was rotten.
She ate it & hated it
& would not go down.
No seasons off for Persephone,
stuck with her mother
like seeds between teeth.

"HAPPY SOULS WHOM DEVILS LIVE SO NEAR"

who can follow Persephone down
the cold river of her hair,
and kiss her other cheek in spring.

A syrup of darkness pours down my throat.
I am not grateful for the horrors
I already know.

Border Control

The local fascist organization in Riga, Perkonkrusts, had stated a policy of annihilation of the Jews in the 1930s.

Secret Order Number One was issued on June 29th, 1941, by the Nazi Chief Department of Imperial Security (RSHA). It mandated that "local circles of self-defence could not allude to [German] orders or political guarantees." Margers Vestermanis, *The Jews in Riga*. Museum and Documentation Centre of the Latvian Society of Jewish Culture, 1991, 25.

from CIRCE, AFTER HOURS

To My Poem of Hope

In 1939, German Jews were required to fill out minority registration forms. These can be viewed at the United States Holocaust Memorial Museum in Washington, D.C.

The prayerbook is housed in the Rexingen Jewish archives. Dr. Gilya Schmidt translated the inscription.

In 1941, the Nazis murdered 26,500 Latvian Jews in the Riga ghetto to make room for transports of more than 20,000 Jews from the Reich and elsewhere (1941–1942). Only a few hundred survived.

Survivor

Many details in this poem were provided by Bernhard Sayer, the archivist for Jewish history for Rexingen/Horb, in a personal interview, March 22, 2004.

"The Night of Broken Glass, *Kristallnacht,* was a state-sanctioned pogrom that took place across Germany on November 8 and 9, 1938.

Some data in the second stanza is from *Pinkas Hakehillot,* "Germany" Yad Vashem, Jerusalem, 1986, 76–78.

Mezuzah

Mezuzah, a small prayer scroll housed in protective casing, is nailed to the right doorpost as a sign of a Jewish home, to invite God's blessing. The prayers include the *Sh'ema* ("Hear, O Israel") and passages from *Deuteronomy:* (6:4–9), (11:13–21). *Judenhausen* were the "Jews' Houses." Their own properties had been confiscated and many families were pushed together in a few houses in Horb.

TITLES FROM BLACK WIDOW PRESS

I Want No Part in It and Other Writings by Benjamin Péret
Translated with an introduction by James Brook. *(Forthcoming)*

Essential Poems and Writings of Jules Laforgue *(Forthcoming)*
Translated and edited by Patricia Terry.

Preversities: A Jacques Prevert Sampler *(Forthcoming)*
Translated and edited by Norman R. Shapiro.

MODERN POETRY SERIES

An Alchemist with One Eye on Fire by Clayton Eshleman

Archaic Design by Clayton Eshleman

Backscatter: New and Selected Poems by John Olson

Crusader-Woman by Ruxandra Cesereanu
Translated by Adam J. Sorkin. Introduction by Andrei Codrescu.

The Grindstone of Rapport: A Clayton Eshleman Reader
Forty years of poetry, prose, and translations by Clayton Eshleman.

Packing Light: New and Selected Poems by Marilyn Kallet

Forgiven Submarine by Ruxandra Cesereanu and Andrei Codrescu
(Forthcoming)

Caveat Onus by Dave Brinks *(Forthcoming)*
Complete cycle, four volumes combined.

Fire Exit by Robert Kelly *(Forthcoming)*

NEW POETS SERIES

Signal from Draco: New and Selected Poems by Mebane Robertson

LITERARY THEORY/BIOGRAPHY SERIES

Revolution of the Mind: The Life of André Breton by Mark Polizzotti
Revised and augmented edition. *(Forthcoming)*

WWW.BLACKWIDOWPRESS.COM